Th
EARTHS CICLE
OF CELEBRATION

The Earths Cycle of Celebration

Publisher: Glennie Kindred
Leamoor · Derby rd · Wirksworth ·
Derbyshire. DE4 4AR.
Tel: 01629 825675/07990 553270

Printed on recycled paper by
4 sheets design and print.
197 Mansfield rd. Nottingham. NG1 3FS.

Wholesale distribution by
Counter Culture. The Long Barn.
Sutton Mallet. Somerset. TA7 9AD.
Tel: 01278 722888.

ISBN: 0-9532227-3-X
Revised edition 2002.

Written and illustrated by Glennie Kindred.

See back for details of other publications
by Glennie Kindred, available from her at
publishers address.

THE EARTHS CYCLE OF CELEBRATION

WRITTEN AND ILLUSTRATED
BY
GLENNIE KINDRED

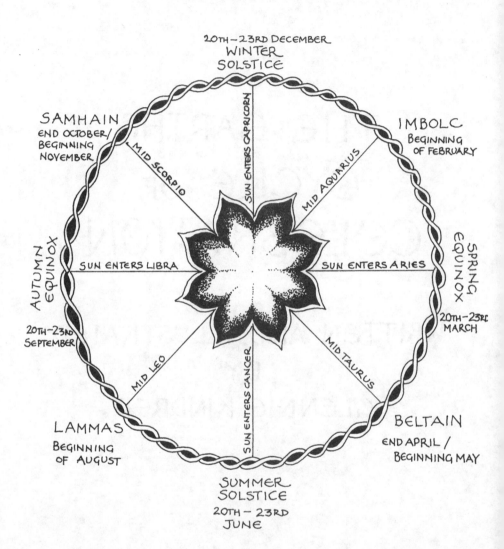

20TH–23RD DECEMBER
WINTER
SOLSTICE

SUN ENTERS CAPRICORN

SAMHAIN
END OCTOBER/
BEGINNING
NOVEMBER

IMBOLC
BEGINNING
OF FEBRUARY

MID SCORPIO

MID AQUARIUS

AUTUMN EQUINOX

SUN ENTERS LIBRA

SUN ENTERS ARIES

SPRING EQUINOX

20TH–23RD
SEPTEMBER

20TH–23RD
MARCH

MID LEO

MID TAURUS

SUN ENTERS CANCER

LAMMAS
BEGINNING
OF AUGUST

BELTAIN
END APRIL /
BEGINNING MAY

SUMMER
SOLSTICE
20TH – 23RD
JUNE

4.

THE WHEEL OF THE YEAR

The Celtic people of our land celebrated the Earth's cyclic flow, by dividing the year into eight divisions. Eight festivals to honour the Earth Mother, to sing, dance and reflect, to come together as a community. These celebrations brought sharing and focus, and it gave structure to their lives.

The wheel of the year is not just a matter of changing from one season to the next. Beneath the manifestation of seasonal change, there is also change in the energy of the Earth. These energy patterns affect us all whether we are conscious of them or not. By understanding the flow and direction of that energy, we can move with it, in harmony with it, as true inhabitants of our planet Earth: belonging, part of, changing on all levels of our being.

This eightfold sub-division of the year is marked by the Solstices, the two exact points in the year when the day/night are longest or shortest (mid-summer and mid-winter) and the two Equinoxes (Spring and Autumn) when day and night are equal in length. These are the quarter points. These are then crossed again by what are known as the Cross-Quarters. The Cross-Quarters are the Four Great Fire Festivals of the Earth's cycle of celebration. They fall at the seasonal peaks and are used to participate with the developing energies of the Earth's natural flow.

THE QUARTER POINTS
WINTER and SUMMER SOLSTICE

The Sun's cycle waxes and wanes over the course of a year. It reaches a peak at each solstice, stops and begins a change in direction, which affects all life on the Earth.

The solstices are a time to stop, to look back on where the half-yearly cycle has brought you, and to look forward to how you will use the developing energy.

When the light is increasing from Winter Solstice to Summer Solstice, all beings are expressing themselves out in the world, celebrating their own identity and uniqueness. But as the light is decreasing from Summer Solstice to Winter Solstice, nature and life as a whole is integrating itself into a more social way of life, going within, exploring inner wisdom and inner truth.

SPRING and AUTUMN EQUINOX

Day and night are equal length. The outer and inner worlds, light and dark, are equal and balanced. This happens twice a year and they provide an opportunity for us to work with this integration within ourselves.

The equinoxes fall at the beginning of two seasonal changes: Spring with its promise of Summer, and Autumn with its promise of Winter. Everything is beginning to move fast at this time. Use these points as a focus for the direction you wish to go. This means you will meet the new season prepared and clear.

THE CROSS QUARTERS

THE QUARTER POINTS OF THE SOLSTICES AND EQUINOXES ARE THEN CROSSED AGAIN MAKING 4 CROSS QUARTER FESTIVALS: IMBOLC, BELTAIN, LAMMAS AND SAMHAIN. EACH OF THESE FESTIVALS FALL AT EACH SEASONAL PEAK, AT THE POINT WHEN THE ENERGY IS ABOUT TO CHANGE. THIS OFFERS A UNIQUE OPPORTUNITY FOR US TO CELEBRATE AND BE AWARE OF THE DEVELOPING ENERGY AND WHAT THIS COULD MEAN FOR US; TO BRING ABOUT MANIFESTATION THROUGH THE POWER OF OUR DEEPEST WISHES AND POSITIVE INTENT. WE CAN WORK WITH THE EARTH'S ENERGY, PARTICIPATING IN A PROCESS OF POSITIVE CHANGE BOTH FOR OURSELVES AND THE EARTH.

EACH OF THE CROSS-QUARTER POINTS IS INFLUENCED BY EACH OF THE 4 ELEMENTS THROUGH THE 4 FIXED ASTROLOGICAL SIGNS. THE FIXED SIGNS ARE STRONG AND ENERGETIC. THEY PROPEL PROJECTS TO COMPLETION:

MID AQUARIUS ♒ FIXED AIR — IMBOLC
MID TAURUS ♉ FIXED EARTH — BELTAIN
MID LEO ♌ FIXED FIRE — LAMMAS
MID SCORPIO ♏ FIXED WATER — SAMHAIN.

THERE ARE SOME WHO WOULD FIX THESE CROSS-QUARTER FESTIVALS BY DATES ON THE CALENDER, BUT I PREFER TO LOOK AT THE POSITION OF THE MOON AND ANY OTHER ASTROLOGICAL INFORMATION AND CHOOSE A TIME WHEN THESE INFLUENCES ARE AT THEIR MOST POTENT. CELEBRATING THE CROSS-QUARTERS MAY LAST SEVERAL DAYS. THEY WERE KNOWN AS THE FOUR GREAT FIRE FESTIVALS, AND IN THE PAST COMMUNITY FIRES WERE LIT ON THE HILLTOPS, UNITING PEOPLE BY A COMMON BOND OF CELEBRATION.

7.

CREATING CEREMONY

OBSERVING THE EIGHT CELTIC FESTIVALS CREATES AN OPPORTUNITY FOR PARTICIPATION IN A CONTINUOUS ONGOING CYCLIC PROCESS. THROUGH CEREMONY WE CAN CONNECT TO OUR INNERMOST FEELINGS, AWARENESS AND NEEDS. THROUGH CEREMONY WE CAN CONSCIOUSLY SEEK THE DIRECTION WE WISH TO GO, BRINGING OUR PHYSICAL AND SPIRITUAL LIVES INTO BALANCE, HELPING US CONNECT TO OUR INTUITION, INNER WISDOM AND PERSONAL POWER.

WHEN PLANNING A CEREMONY, TAKE INTO ACCOUNT THE SEASON, WHO IS COMING, AND THE TYPE OF VENUE. DO NOT TRY TO DO TOO MUCH, THE SIMPLEST THINGS WORK BEST AS THEY CAN BE INTERPRETED ON MANY LEVELS. ALLOW FOR SPONTANEITY AND THE GREATEST FREEDOM OF EXPRESSION AND PARTICIPATION BY THE WHOLE GROUP. FIND WAYS TO INCLUDE THE CHILDREN.

BEGIN BY CREATING SACRED SPACE, BOTH WITHIN YOURSELF AND THE PLACE YOU WILL USE. LIGHT A CANDLE, FIND YOUR STILLNESS, STATE YOUR INTENT, ASK FOR GUIDANCE FROM YOUR SPIRIT GUIDES AND GUARDIAN ANGELS. CLEANSE THE SPACE USING SALT, BURNING HERBS AND INCENSE, ESTABLISH THE 5 DIRECTIONS: AIR IN THE EAST, FIRE IN

8.

THE SOUTH, WATER IN
THE WEST, EARTH IN
THE NORTH AND SPIRIT
AT THE CENTRE.

OPENING AND CLOSING A CEREMONY

AN OPENING CEREMONY PROVIDES THE
FOCUS FOR THE CELEBRATION TO BEGIN.
IF YOU ARE CELEBRATING WITH A GROUP
OF PEOPLE, IT BRINGS THE GROUP
TOGETHER. DRUMBEAT, CHANTING, MUSIC,
CIRCLE DANCE, WILL HELP CHANGE THE
ATMOSPHERE AND STILL THE MIND.
WHEN THIS HAS HAPPENED, DECLARE THE
INTENTION, THE REASON FOR THE CEREMONY.
WELCOME ALL PRESENT, SEEN AND UNSEEN.
WELCOME AND THANK THE 5 ELEMENTS, AIR,
FIRE, WATER, EARTH AND SPIRIT. WELCOME
THE PRESENCE OF YOUR SPIRIT GUIDES, SPIRIT
HELPERS, GUARDIAN ANGELS AND THE ANCESTORS.
ONCE THIS IS DONE, THEN A FOCUSED ACTIVITY
CAN FOLLOW TO HELP YOU CONNECT TO THE
MOMENT. USE YOUR IMAGINATION SO THAT
WHAT YOU CREATE HAS MEANING FOR YOU.
I HOPE THE IDEAS I HAVE OFFERED WILL
HELP INSPIRE YOU.
WHATEVER IS OPENED MUST BE CLOSED.
FOLLOW THE FOCUSED ACTIVITY WITH A
CLOSING CEREMONY, THANKING ALL
PRESENT, SEEN AND UNSEEN.
THIS CAN ALSO BE DONE
ANY TIME LATER.

THE FIVE ELEMENTS

THE FIVE ELEMENTS FORM THE WHOLE.
INVOKE THEM, INVITE THEM, WELCOME THEM,
THANK THEM, FEEL THEM WITHIN YOURSELF, AS
WELL AS PART OF ALL EXISTENCE. ACKNOWLEDGE
THEM IN ANY WAY WHICH FEELS GOOD AND MAKES A
TRUE HEARTFELT CONNECTION. VISUALIZE THEM
STRONGLY IN YOUR MIND. THIS CREATES LINKS AND
CONNECTORS FOR THE ENERGY TO TRAVEL THROUGH.

MARK AND STAND AT THE CENTRE AND FIND YOUR
STILL POINT WITHIN. WHEN YOU ARE READY, PLACE
A COMPASS AT THE CENTRE, TURN IT UNTIL THE
RED ARROW IS ON NORTH. THIS ESTABLISHES THE
FOUR DIRECTIONS. MARK THEM WITH A STONE, OR
SYMBOLIC REPRESENTATION FOR EACH, IE; A CRYSTAL
IN THE NORTH, A FEATHER OR BELL IN THE EAST, A
CANDLE OR INCENSE IN THE SOUTH, A BOWL OF WATER
IN THE WEST. LIGHT A SPECIAL CANDLE AT THE
CENTRE.

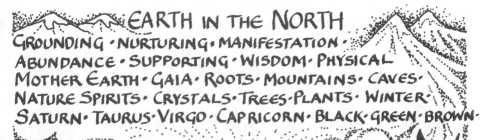

EARTH IN THE NORTH

GROUNDING · NURTURING · MANIFESTATION ·
ABUNDANCE · SUPPORTING · WISDOM · PHYSICAL
MOTHER EARTH · GAIA · ROOTS · MOUNTAINS · CAVES ·
NATURE SPIRITS · CRYSTALS · TREES · PLANTS · WINTER ·
SATURN · TAURUS · VIRGO · CAPRICORN · BLACK · GREEN · BROWN ·

WATER
IN THE WEST

THE EMOTIONS ·
MEMORY · LOVE ·
THE UNCONSCIOUS ·
RECEPTIVITY ·
COMPASSION ·
CLEANSING ·
HEALING ·
FLOW ·
THE HEART ·
THE TIDES ·
AUTUMN ·
SUNSET ·
THE MOON ·
PLUTO ·
NEPTUNE ·
SCORPIO ·
PISCES · BLUE ·
PURPLE ·

SPIRIT
AT THE
CENTRE
AND ALL
AROUND ·
WITHIN US ·
BEYOND US ·
ABOVE & BELOW
CONNECTING ·
UNIVERSAL LOVE ·
EVER PRESENT ·
THE SOURCE ·
INFINITE ·
TIMELESS ·
ONENESS ·
THE
IS
·

AIR
IN THE EAST

NEW BEGINNINGS ·
COMMUNICATION ·
THOUGHTS ·
THE MIND ·
INSPIRATION ·
RENEWAL ·
REBIRTH ·
MESSAGES ·
VISION ·
THE VOICE ·
SOUND · BIRDS ·
FLIGHT · WIND ·
THE DAWN ·
SPRING · VENUS ·
MERCURY · URANUS ·
GEMINI · AQUARIUS ·
LIBRA · WHITE · YELLOW ·

FIRE IN THE SOUTH

TRANSFORMATION · CHANGE · THE WILL ·
PURIFYING · EXPANSIVE · ACTIVE · SPONTANEITY ·
CREATIVITY · PASSION · COURAGE · SEXUALITY ·
GROWTH · MID-DAY · SUMMER · JUPITER · MARS ·
THE SUN · SAGITTARIUS · ARIES · LEO ·
RED · ORANGE · GOLD ·

Winter Solstice
21st – 23rd December
Winter Quarter Point
Shortest Day / Longest Night
Midwinter · Yule
Return of the Sun
Festival of Rebirth

The Sun enters the sign of Capricorn ♑ as her rays shine directly at their southern extreme for the year. In the Northern Hemisphere, the shortest day and longest night. Here the great cosmic wheel stops and begins again a new cycle of increasing daylight and warmth.

Underlying Energy

This festival is not a beginning in a linear sense, but part of a cycle. Deep within the earth and ourselves, roots have been growing, bringing stability. The outer world has darkened and the inner realms can expand. But here there is a change in direction. From now on the days will lengthen. Being part of this cycle means that we can bring our inner wisdom out of the dark unconscious, to grow with the increasing light. It is a time to birth our visions, name our dreams and make our resolutions for the coming months.

Winter Solstice is an opportunity to come out of hibernation, be loving, generous and sociable. Celebrate eachother and being alive.

The old year has died and the way is now prepared for the rebirth of activity and expansion into the outer world.

12.

13.

WINTER SOLSTICE CELEBRATIONS

⊙ MAKE A WHEEL OF EVERGREENS TO REPRESENT EVERLASTING LIFE. YEW, HOLLY, PINE, MISTLETOE AND IVY ALL HAVE TRADITIONAL SYMBOLISM. USE WILLOW WHIPS TO MAKE THE BASE.

⊙ CUT EVERGREENS AND SEED HEADS TO MAKE A SOLSTICE BUSH, PUSHING THE STALKS INTO A LARGE POT OF WET SOIL.

⊙ DECORATE A LOG OF OAK AND PLACE ON THE FIRE WITH CEREMONY, RELEASING THE PAST. LEAVE BEHIND WHAT IS NO LONGER HELPFUL TO YOU. RELEASING OLD ENERGY OPENS THE WAY FOR NEW ENERGY TO COME IN.

⊙ BE STILL. EXPERIENCE THE STILLNESS. BE AWARE OF WHERE YOU ARE PHYSICALLY, MENTALLY, AND SPIRITUALLY, AND THE DIRECTION YOU WISH TO GO IN.

⊙ EACH LIGHT A CANDLE AND SPEAK OUT YOUR WISHES, HOPES AND INTENTIONS. PLACE IN A LARGE BOWL OF SAND OR SOIL AND LET THEM BURN RIGHT DOWN.

⊙ GATHER TOGETHER WITH FAMILY, FRIENDS AND KIN. EXPERIENCE BELONGING TO THE WHOLE. BE GENEROUS, LOVING AND GIVING. WRAP UP UNWANTED POSSESSIONS, PLACE IN A BASKET SO EACH CAN CHOOSE A GIFT. BRING SPECIAL FOOD AND DRINK TO SHARE AND HAVE A FEAST. PARTY, DANCE, SING, TELL STORIES, ENTERTAIN EACH OTHER.

⊙ JOURNEY WITHIN TO MEET YOUR SPIRIT GUIDE, GUARDIAN ANGEL, OR TOTEM ANIMAL GUIDE. STATE YOUR INTENTION TO WORK WITH THEM. ASK FOR THEIR GUIDANCE AND INNER CLARITY.

STANDING IN THE CIRCLE
BENEATH THE WEB OF LIGHT
DANCING IN THE MOONLIGHT
ON A COLD NEW YEAR'S NIGHT
AND IT SEEMED THAT WE WERE LIFTED
FLOWN ACROSS THE YEARS
POWER-CIRCLE SHIFTED, BY POWER-CIRCLE SEERS

AND THE GODDESS AND JOHN BARLEYCORN
WILL PUT FLESH UPON THE BONES
FLY RIBBONS ROUND THE BARROWS
PLANT FOOT PRINTS ROUND THE STONES
THE GODDESS AND JOHN BARLEYCORN
WILL KEEP THE SPIRIT STRONG
FOR THOSE WHO REMEMBER
FOR THOSE WHO SING THE SONG

SO STAND IN THE CIRCLE, WEAVE THE WEB OF LIGHT
DANCE IN THE MOONLIGHT
BRING FIRE TO THE NIGHT
RELEASE THE PAST THAT MADE US
RELEASE THE FIRE WITHIN
REVEL IN THE MYSTERY
AND EMBRACE YOUR
SACRED KIN

BY BRIAN BOOTHBY.

IMBOLC
END JANUARY
BEGIN FEBRUARY
WINTER CROSS-QUARTER
CANDLEMAS · BRIGIDS DAY · IMOLG
DIVINE SPARK · NEW MOON
FESTIVAL OF EARTH AWAKENING

THIS IS A CELEBRATION OF THE LIFE-FORCE. PERSEPHONE RETURNS FROM THE UNDERWORLD (THE INNER WORLD) AS HERSELF MADE NEW. IN CELTIC TRADITION THE TRIPLE GODDESS HAS BECOME HER VIRGIN SELF AGAIN, BRIDE, BRIGID, BRIGIT, THE MAIDEN. HER ATTRIBUTES ARE INTUITION, INSPIRATION, DIVINATION, HEALING, KEEPER OF THE SACRED FIRE, THE SPARK OF LIFE. HER LIFE-GIVING WATERS ARE THE SACRED SPRINGS AND HOLY WELLS OF OUR LAND. SHE IS THE PRESERVER OF TRADITION AND CHANNELLED ANCESTRAL MEMORY, THROUGH POETRY AND SONG. THIS IS A TIME FOR VISION AND CLAIRVOYANCE.

HERE WE CAN USE THE INNER WISDOM WE HAVE GAINED DURING THE WINTER MONTHS AND BRING IT OUT INTO THE ACTIVE PART OF THE YEAR. THE SPARK OF INTUITION AND THE INTELLECT OF CONSCIOUSNESS JOIN TOGETHER TO BRING ABOUT FERTILITY AND GROWTH ON ALL LEVELS. THIS UNION OF THE TWO ASPECTS OF OURSELVES CREATES A MAGICAL AND FERTILE TIME, A TIME OF AWAKENINGS AND NEW BEGINNINGS, CHARGED WITH THE POTENCY OF RISING ENERGY.

THIS FESTIVAL IS SACRED TO LOVE, (HENCE ITS PROXIMITY TO VALENTINE'S DAY), AND ESPECIALLY TO WOMEN. HERE WE CAN CELEBRATE THE RE-EMERGENCE OF THE SERPENT, KUNDALINI, THE LIFE-FORCE, THE DOUBLE HELIX, THE DNA. IT IS INTRINSICALLY LINKED TO INNER WISDOM, HEALING AND THE SACRED POWER OF SEXUALITY.

16.

UNDERLYING ENERGY of IMBOLC

As with all Cross-Quarter Festivals, this is the point when the manifest energy begins to change. We can use this time to activate our new cycle.

Our acceptance of winter is giving way to an urge to move forward into Springtime energy. Now is the time to prepare inwardly for the changes which will come. Plant your visions and ideas, leave them to germinate. Bring forth your inner understanding through poetry, song art and craftwork. Divination and clairvoyance are potent now as the link with the inner realms remains strong.

This is the time for initiation and healing, for reclaiming what has been forgotten. A time for working with your intuition, inspired leaps of faith, expressing your deepest feelings and understanding your own inner wisdom and beliefs. From your unconscious many things will be revealed to bring understanding of yourself. This is the special energy of Imbolc which will help you find your way forward.

IMBOLC CELEBRATIONS

◊ GATHER AT NEWMOON TO SHARE VISIONS, DREAMS, POEMS AND SONGS.

◊ MEDITATE AND CONNECT TO THE RE-EMERGING POWER WHICH IS STIRRING DEEP IN THE EARTH. ASK FOR GUIDANCE FROM WITHIN AND FROM YOUR SPIRIT GUIDES. USE DIVINATION SYSTEMS TO SEEK DIRECTION.

◊ THIS IS THE TIME FOR ANY RITE OF PASSAGE OR INITIATION CEREMONY. CREATE YOUR OWN, ENCOMPASSING THREE PHASES: SEPARATION FROM THE OLD, A TRANSITION, AND INTEGRATION INTO THE NEW.

◊ COLLECT SNOWDROPS AND FRESH LEAVES FOR YOUR SHRINE. GATHER TWIGS OF WILLOW, FORSYTHIA, WINTER JASMIN, ALMOND AND CHERRY BUDS. WEAVE THEM TOGETHER INTO A CIRCLE AND PLACE THIS IN A SHALLOW DISH OF WATER. OVER THE NEXT FEW WEEKS FRESH GROWTH AND FLOWERS WILL COME OUT.

◊ LIGHT A FIRE OR LOTS OF CANDLES. USE THE FIRE TO CLEANSE AND TRANSFORM WHAT YOU WISH TO LEAVE BEHIND, WHAT IS NO LONGER HELPFUL TO YOU. THIS OPENS THE WAY FOR NEW BEGINNINGS AND YOUR OWN NEW GROWTH.

◊ LIGHT CANDLES FOR THOSE WHO YOU LOVE AND FOR YOURSELF. AFFIRM THE POSITIVE QUALITIES IN ALL YOUR RELATIONSHIPS.

◊ DRUM AND DANCE TO ACTIVATE AND CONNECT TO THE FIRE WITHIN. FEEL THE LIFE-FORCE RISING INSIDE YOU AND THE EARTH.

◊ USE SEEDS OR CRYSTALS TO SYMBOLICALLY PLANT IDEAS, SEEDS OF FUTURE INTENT. SHARE THESE WITH EACH OTHER. AFFIRM NEW DIRECTIONS IN YOUR LIFE. CELEBRATE YOUR EMERGING SELF, YOUR ACCOMPLISHMENTS AND EACH OTHER'S.

SPRING EQUINOX
21st – 22nd MARCH
SPRING QUARTER POINT
DAY AND NIGHT EQUAL LENGTH
OESTAR · OESTRE · EASTER
FESTIVAL OF BALANCE and AWAKENING

KNOWN IN THE NORTHERN HEMISPHERE AS THE
FIRST DAY OF SPRING. THE BALANCE OF DAY AND
NIGHT, LIGHT AND DARK, INNER AND OUTER, INTUITION
AND RATIONAL, CONSCIOUS AND UNCONSCIOUS,
FEMALE AND MALE. THIS BRINGS FERTILITY AND
MANIFESTATION ON ALL LEVELS. PLANS WHICH
HAVE BEEN INCUBATING ON THE INNER LEVELS
SINCE AUTUMN EQUINOX CAN NOW HATCH OUT
ONTO THE PHYSICAL PLANE. THE EGG IS A POTENT
SYMBOL HERE, FULL OF POTENTIAL AND NEW
LIFE. A TIME TO CELEBRATE THE FERTILE GODDESS
OESTRE (THE ROOT OF THE WORD OESTROGEN, THE
HORMONE STIMULATING OVULATION), THE UNION OF
OPPOSITES, THE BLENDING OF FEMALE AND MALE
WITHIN OURSELVES REGARDLESS OF GENDER. HERE
THE DRAGON WAS GIVEN A GOOD WELCOME IN, BRINGING
AWARENESS OF THE ACTIVE EARTH ENERGY.

UNDERLYING ENERGY

EVERYTHING IN NATURE IS COMING ALIVE. THE SUN
IS GAINING STRENGTH AND THE DAYS ARE LONGER
AND WARMER. IT IS THE TIME TO THROW OFF THE
RESTRAINTS OF WINTER AND REACH OUT FOR WHAT
WE WANT, MAKE PLANS, JOURNEY FORTH, TAKE RISKS.
THE EARTH'S ENERGIES ARE NOW BLENDED. CELEBRATE
THE DANCE OF LIFE, OF GAIA — INTERDEPENDENT
COMPLEMENTARY PARTS OF ONE ENERGY SYSTEM
WHICH WE CAN EMBRACE ON OUR JOURNEY TO
20.   BECOME WHOLE.

SPRING EQUINOX
CELEBRATIONS

θ BE OUTSIDE ALL DAY. WRAP UP WARM. ENJOY THE ELEMENTS. RUN WILD. SENSE THE AWAKENING NATURE SPIRITS.

θ CREATE A SHRINE TO EQUINOX USING SPRING FLOWERS, BUDS, BLOSSOM. GIVE THANKS FOR NEW DIRECTIONS. AFFIRM YOUR MOST POSITIVE INTENT AND WISHES.

θ DECORATE HARD BOILED EGGS AND ROLL THEM DOWN A HILL OR EAT THEM AS PART OF YOUR CELEBRATION. HANG DECORATED BLOWN EGGS IN YOUR WINDOW OR MAKE A NEST FOR THEM.

θ MAKE FLAGS, KITES OR OTHER FLYING THINGS TO RUN WITH IN THE WIND. THEY CAN CARRY YOUR PRAYERS, WISHES AND VISIONS.

θ GIVE SPRING-CLEANING A NEW MEANING AS YOU CLEANSE YOUR SPACE WITH POSITIVE INTENT. PUT SALT IN YOUR CLEANING WATER TO AID PHSYCIC CLEANSING. BANISH OLD PATTERNS, OLD ENERGY AND INVOKE THE NEW. GIVE AWAY AND CHANGE WHAT IS HOLDING YOU BACK.

θ PLANT SEEDS OF HERBS AND FUTURE FOOD. EACH BRING SEEDS TO SHARE WITH EACHOTHER. PAINT AND DECORATE PLANT POTS.

θ PLANT THE SEEDS OF YOURSELF AND LOOK AT WHERE YOU ARE GOING NOW.

θ PASS A CRYSTAL EGG AROUND THE CIRCLE. SHARE WITH EACH OTHER WHAT YOU WISH TO BRING OUT INTO THE WORLD.

θ MAKE A DRAGON. DANCE A DRAGON DANCE.

θ LOOK FOR THE ANCIENT PATHWAYS, THE LEY-LINES OR DRAGON PATHS, AS THEIR ENERGY BECOMES FULLY ACTIVE AT THIS TIME OF THE YEAR. SPEND TIME IN PLACES OF POWER. EARTH ENERGY IS STRONG NOW.

21.

THE KISS.

BELTAIN
END APRIL BEGIN MAY
SPRING CROSS-QUARTER
BEL-TENE · WALPURGISNACHT · MAY EVE / MAY DAY · FULL MOON · FESTIVAL OF FERTILITY

BELTAIN CELEBRATES THE FERTILITY OF THE EARTH AND THE POTENCY OF THE LIFE-FORCE. IN THE PAST IT WAS THE NIGHT OF THE GREENWOOD MARRIAGE, WHEN THE UNION BETWEEN THE HORNED GOD AND THE FERTILE GODDESS WAS RE-ENACTED BY THE WOMEN AND MEN TO ENSURE THE FERTILITY OF THE LAND. THROUGH THEIR UNION, THEIR KNOWLEGE AND POWER IS SHARED AND THEY BECOME THE FERTILE FORCE OF MANIFEST ENERGY.

THIS WAS THE BEGINNING OF THE 'MERRY-MONTH', WHEN PEOPLE DRESSED IN GREEN IN HONOUR OF THE EARTH'S NEW COLOUR AND THE FAERIE FOLK, ELEMENTALS AND NATURE SPIRITS WHO ARE EASIER TO MEET AT THIS TIME.

THE TEIN-EIGIN, THE NEED-FIRE, WAS A SACRED FIRE, KINDLED AFTER ALL THE OTHER FIRES IN THE COMMUNITY HAD BEEN PUT OUT. PEOPLE JUMPED THIS FIRE TO BRING FERTILITY, HEALING, TRANSFORMATION, AND TO PLEDGE THEMSELVES TO EACHOTHER.

MAY-EVE WAS A NIGHT TO BE OUT IN THE WILDWOODS. PEOPLE WALKED THE LABYRINTHS AND SLEPT BY THE WELLS, WHICH WERE SAID TO BE ESPECIALLY HEALING AT THIS TIME. RIBBONS AND GIFTS WERE HUNG IN THE HAWTHORN TREES. ON MAY MORNING PEOPLE DANCED AROUND THE MAYPOLE, SYMBOLIZING JOINING FEMALE AND MALE ENERGY.

A TIME FOR FRIENDS AND LOVERS AND HONOURING UNIONS OF ALL KINDS.

23.

UNDERLYING ENERGY of BELTAIN

This is the beginning of the final and most actively potent part of the cycle. All of life is bursting with fertility and the power of its potential. This is the peak of the Spring season and the beginning of the Summer, when the Earth is clothed in green, the vibration of the Heart chakra and love. Everywhere Life is manifesting itself and moving outwards.

The Earth's energies are at their most active now, and the same as at Samhain, the veil between the worlds is thin. At dawn and dusk especially, we may slip through from our known reality to touch the realms of Faerie and commune with nature spirits.

Beltain energy is one of reverence for all of life. Reach out for what it is you want. Everything is possible.

BELTAIN CELEBRATIONS

◎ THE FIRE IS CENTRAL TO THIS CELEBRATION. ASK EVERYONE TO BRING WOOD. LEAP THE FIRE WITH FRIENDS AND LOVERS. HONOUR UNIONS OF ALL KINDS. MAKE A PLEDGE AS YOU JUMP! 'I PLEDGE MYSELF TO....' LEAVE BEHIND WHAT IS NO LONGER HELPING YOU 'I LEAVE BEHIND......'

◎ WEAR MASKS OR CROWNS OR HEAD-DRESSES OF GREENERY. WEAR GREEN IN HONOUR OF THE EARTH'S NEW COLOUR, FAERIE, THE GREEN MAN, NATURE SPIRITS, DRYADS, ELEMENTALS.

◎ USING DRUMBEAT AND CHANT, CIRCLE THE FIRE. FOCUS ON BLESSING AND NAMING MANIFEST UNIONS AND DIRECTIONS YOU WANT.

◎ DANCE AROUND A MAYPOLE OR A TREE OR A TREE IN A POT. INTERWEAVING DANCES WILL ENHANCE THE SPIRIT OF UNION.

◎ THANK ALL OF NATURE, ESPECIALLY THE TREES FOR ALL THEIR GIFTS TO HUMANKIND. HANG RIBBONS IN THEIR BRANCHES AS YOU MAKE A WISH OR A BLESSING. BLESS AND DRESS THE WELLS OR A LOCAL SPRING

◎ STAY OUTSIDE ALL NIGHT AND EXPERIENCE THE MAGIC OF THE DAWN. WASH YOUR FACE IN THE MORNING DEW.

◎ NOW IS THE TIME TO BE CLEAR ABOUT YOUR DIRECTION AND WHAT YOU WILL USE THIS GROWTH PERIOD FOR. CELEBRATE YOUR POTENTIAL AND SHARE YOUR PLANS AND DESIRES.

◎ CREATE A SPIRAL OR LABYRINTH IN SALT. LET GO OF OLD RESTRAINTS AS YOU WALK TO THE CENTRE. AT THE CENTRE, ASK A QUESTION, SEEK YOUR DIRECTION AND BRING THIS NEW INSIGHT OUT WITH YOU.

26.

SUMMER SOLSTICE

SUMMER QUARTER POINT
20TH-23RD JUNE
MID-SUMMER
ST JOHNS DAY · LITHA ·
LONGEST DAY AND SHORTEST NIGHT
FESTIVAL OF ATTAINMENT · RETURN OF THE DARK

THE SUN ENTERS THE SIGN OF CANCER, AS HER RAYS SHINE DOWN ON EARTH DIRECTLY AT THE FARTHEST POINT NORTH IN THE ANNUAL CYCLE (TROPIC OF CANCER). IN THE NORTHERN HEMISPHERE, THE LONGEST DAY AND THE SHORTEST NIGHT. THE SUN REACHES THE HEIGHT OF ITS POWER, BUT NOW AT THIS OTHER GREAT TURNING POINT OF THE YEAR, THE ENERGY CHANGES. THE DAYS WILL BEGIN TO SHORTEN AND THE SUN'S POWER WILL BEGIN TO WANE. ON MIDSUMMER EVE, FIRES WERE LIT ON HILL TOPS. PEOPLE STAYED UP ALL NIGHT TO WATCH THE SUNRISE. A NIGHT FOR CARNIVAL AND CANDLELIT PROCESSIONS. THIS IS A DUAL CELEBRATION, HONOURING THE LIGHT AND ALL THAT IS MANIFEST, AND THE RETURN OF THE DARK SIDE OF THE YEAR, CONNECTING ONCE AGAIN TO THE INNER WORLD.

UNDERLYING ENERGY

THE RAMPANT GROWTH PERIOD HAS REACHED ITS PEAK. EVERYWHERE THERE IS A SENSE OF ABUNDANCE AND FRESH GROWTH. THIS IS THE PEAK OF OUR EXPRESSIVE AND EXPANSIVE SELVES. CELEBRATE ALL OF YOUR ACHIEVEMENTS AND WHO YOU ARE.

BUT A GREAT TRANSITION IS BEGINNING WHICH WILL BRING A COMPLETION OF OUR WHOLESELVES. THE POWER OF THE INNER REALMS WILL BEGIN TO EXPAND AND OUR ACHIEVEMENTS WILL RIPEN WITHIN.

27.

SUMMER SOLSTICE CELEBRATIONS

☀ STAY UP ALL NIGHT ON SOLSTICE-EVE AND WATCH THE SUN RISE.

☀ CELEBRATE THE SUN AND ITS GIFTS TO US. CELEBRATE YOURSELF AND YOUR ACHIEVEMENTS.

☀ GATHER WITH FRIENDS FOR A CIRCULAR WALK OR CANDLELIT PROCESSION. CELEBRATE THE WHEEL OF THE YEAR TURNING, REBIRTH AND THE DESCENT INTO THE MYSTERIES.

☀ DECORATE YOURSELVES WITH GARLANDS OF FLOWERS AND HEAD-DRESSES WOVEN FROM FLOWERS AND GRASSES.

☀ CREATE A SHRINE TO THE SUN WHERE EACH CAN LAY A POSY OF FLOWERS WITH A WISH FOR THE COMING ENERGY CHANGE.

☀ TRADITIONALLY, POTTED HERBS WERE GIVEN AS GIFTS TO FRIENDS AT THIS TIME.

☀ CUT GARDEN HERBS, DRY THEM IN THE DARK (BROWN PAPER BAGS ARE GOOD). USE MUSLIN TO MAKE HERB BAGS FOR TEA AND BATHS. (POUR ON BOILING WATER)

☀ PASS AROUND A FRUIT CUP AND TOAST AND CELEBRATE EACH OTHER AT THIS PEAK OF OUTER FULFILLMENT. BE SPONTANEOUS, SING, DANCE, EXPRESS YOURSELF, YOUR HOPES AND INTENTIONS WHILE THERE IS STILL ENERGY LEFT TO USE. BE AWARE OF WHAT THIS WILL MEAN FOR YOU WHEN YOU GO WITHIN.

☀ A TIME FOR OUTDOOR FIRES, FIRESHOWS, AND FIREWORKS. SYMBOLICALLY THROW IN THE FIRE WHAT IS HOLDING YOU BACK. WRITE IT ON A PIECE OF PAPER TO BURN.

☀ THIS IS THE TIME FOR SACRED DRAMA TO EXPLORE GREAT TRUTHS AND THE MYSTERIES.

29.

LAMMAS

END JULY/ BEGINNING AUGUST.

LUGHNASADH
FEAST OF LUGH
HARVEST FULL MOON
SUMMER CROSS-QUARTER FESTIVAL
CELEBRATION OF THE GRAIN-MOTHER
FESTIVAL OF FIRST FRUITS AND REMINDER

THIS IS THE SUMMER'S HEIGHT AND THE CELEBRATION OF THE GRAIN HARVEST. A TIME FOR TRIBAL GATHERING, FEASTING, PLAY AND ASSESSMENT. THE LAST SHEAF OF THE CEREAL CROP AND THE FIRST FRUITS WERE OFFERED TO THE HARVEST MOTHER, THE EARTH MOTHER, CERES, CEREALIA (ROMAN), DEMETER (GREEK), THE INCREASER, THE MOTHER ASPECT OF THE TRIPLE GODDESS, SHE WHO IS THE SEED, WHO IS THE WOMB AND THE SOIL, THE PRESERVER OF LIFE, THE REGENERATIVE POWER, GAIA, GREAT PROVIDER.

DEMETER, THE CORN MOTHER, REPRESENTS THE RIPE CORN OF THIS YEAR'S HARVEST AND HER DAUGHTER KORE/PERSEPHONE REPRESENTS THE GRAIN-SEED WHO LIVES IN THE DARK THROUGHOUT THE WINTER AND RE-APPEARS IN THE SPRING AS NEW GROWTH. THROUGH REST, SLEEP AND TIME IN THE DARK, WE ARE MADE NEW.

THIS WAS THE TIME OF GREAT LAMMAS FAIRS, TRADING FAIRS, HORSE FAIRS AND HORSE RACING — IN HONOUR OF RHIANNON, THE HORSE GODDESS OF THE UNDERWORLD. ALSO THE TIME FOR RITUAL GAMES, MARRIAGES AND THE CHOOSING OF A NEW TRIBAL LEADER.

LUGH OR LUG IS THE CORN KING OR SUN KING WHO DIES WITH THE WANING YEAR. SYMBOLIZING FOR US ALL THE SACRIFICE OF OUR OUTER ENERGY AND AN OPPORTUNITY TO

30.

JOURNEY WITHIN. THIS BRINGS REGENERATION AND
THE RIPENING OF OUR SEEDS IN THE DARK OF THE YEAR.

UNDERLYING ENERGY

LAMMAS IS THE SEASONAL PEAK OF HIGH
SUMMER, AND AS WITH ALL CROSS- QUARTER FESTIVALS
IT IS THE POINT WHEN WE MUST RESPOND TO THE
CHANGES WHICH ARE COMING. THE GRAIN HARVEST IS
BEING GATHERED IN, REPRESENTING FOR US, BOTH THE
FOOD WHICH WILL SUSTAIN US THROUGHOUT THE
WINTER, AND THE SEED, WHICH WILL GROW AGAIN IN
THE SPRING TO BRING NEXT YEAR'S HARVEST.

IT IS A TIME TO GIVE THANKS FOR THE ACTIVE
GROWTH PERIOD AS THE SUN'S ENERGY BEGINS TO
WANE. WE TURN ONCE AGAIN TO FACE OUR INNER
SELVES, ASSIMILATING AND UNDERSTANDING ON
DEEPER LEVELS WHAT WE HAVE MANIFEST.

LAMMAS CELEBRATIONS

TRADITIONALLY A TRIBAL GATHERING AND CELEBRATION OF THE GRAIN HARVEST. GATHER WITH FRIENDS AT THE FULL MOON. LIGHT A FIRE, DANCE IN THE MOONLIGHT, STAY UP UNTIL DAWN.

CREATE A BEAUTIFUL SHRINE TO HONOUR THE GRAIN MOTHER. BAKE BREAD, CAKES AND BISCUITS. LOOK FOR THE FIRST FRUITS.

GIVE THANKS FOR THE GRAIN HARVEST, REMEMBERING ALL THE PEOPLE IN THE WORLD WHO ARE SUFFERING FROM LACK OF FOOD.

WEAVE CORN DOLLIES FROM GRASSES OR GRAIN STALKS. TIE THEM WITH RIBBONS. OR CREATE ONE LARGE CORN MOTHER WHICH CAN BE PARADED OR PLACED CENTRAL WITH LIGHTED CANDLES AROUND HER.

FOCUS ON THE REWARDS YOU ARE HARVESTING. GIVE THANKS FOR YOUR ABUNDANCE. MEDITATE ON THE SEED WITHIN YOUR HARVEST. EVERYTHING CAN BE SEEN IN A POSITIVE LIGHT. COUNT YOUR BLESSINGS.

GATHER TOGETHER OR DANCE IN A CIRCLE. EACH PLACE A POSIE OF FLOWERS AT THE CENTRE, OR EACH LIGHT A CANDLE AND PLACE IN A LARGE DISH OF SOIL. SHARE YOUR HARVEST THANKS AND BLESSINGS.

ASK EVERYONE TO BRING SOMETHING FOR A BASKET OF ABUNDANCE. PUT SOMETHING IN AND TAKE OUT SOMETHING WHICH SOMEONE ELSE HAS PUT IN.

BLESS AND GIVE THANKS FOR ALL THE FOOD AND DRINK BROUGHT TO SHARE. FEAST AND PARTY. PLAY GAMES AND HAVE RACES. NOW IS THE TIME FOR ANY COMMUNITY EVENTS WHICH NEED TO BE MARKED, SUCH AS BABY NAMING OR HANDFASTING (MARRIAGE) ETC.

AUTUMN EQUINOX
20th – 23rd September
AUTUMN QUARTER POINT
ALBAN ELUED · HARVEST ·
DAY and NIGHT EQUAL LENGTH ·
FESTIVAL of THANKSGIVING and RESTORED BALANCE

DAY AND NIGHT ARE IN PERFECT BALANCE AND THE FINAL STAGES OF THE HARVEST ARE COMPLETE. THIS IS THE FAMILY GATHERING OF AUTUMN'S END, THANKSGIVING, HARVEST FESTIVAL, A CELEBRATION OF NATURE'S ABUNDANCE.

UNDERLYING ENERGY

EQUINOXES ARE A CHANCE TO STOP AND ADJUST. THINGS ARE MOVING FAST NOW, PREPARATIONS AND INTENTIONS FOR THE COMING WINTER MUST BE MADE. SUMMER HAS ENDED. THE DAYS WILL SHORTEN. THE COOLER WEATHER REMINDS US THAT WE MUST ALL RESPOND TO THIS TRANSITION AND CHANGE WITH IT. THIS IS THE BEGINNING OF ROOT ENERGY, BRINGING REST AND RENEWAL IN THE DARK. THIS IS THE CHANCE FOR US ALL TO GO WITHIN AND RE-ENTER THE DARK WOMB OF THE SPIRITUAL WORLD. WHICH PROVIDES A STRONG FOUNDATION FOR OUR LIVES, IT IS AN OPPORTUNITY TO EXPLORE AND UNDERSTAND OURSELVES.

THIS IS A TIME OF RIPENING FRUITS, NUTS, BERRIES AND MUSHROOMS. HERE DRAGONS ARE INVOKED TO CARRY THE FIRE ENERGY INTO THE INNER REALMS. IT IS A TIME FOR LONG TERM PLANNING ON THE LAND, MOVING AND PLANTING TREES AND PLANTS.

WITHIN OURSELVES IT IS ALSO A TIME TO PLANT SEEDS, WHICH WILL INCUBATE THROUGH THE WINTER MONTHS AND RE-EMERGE IN THE SPRING, TRANSFORMED AND STRENGTHENED BY THEIR TIME IN THE DARK.

AUTUMN EQUINOX CELEBRATIONS

This is a time to gather with family and friends to celebrate the harvest. Ask everyone to bring seasonal food to share, and nature's abundant gifts to decorate an equinox shrine.

Connect to your inner pathways rest, re-charge, slip out of time dream a while.

Pass round a basket of tree seeds, acorns, hazelnuts, almonds, walnuts, rowan berries etc. Use the seed as a focus for what you wish to grow. You can plant it in compost and leave outside during the winter. A new shoot may surprise you in the spring. This may also be done using spring bulbs.

Have some baskets of yarns, beads, seeds, shells, feathers etc. Make a necklace of power, threading on each thing with a prayer, an intent or affirmation. Walk in the woods and ask to be guided to a special stick or wand. Wrap coloured threads around this, affirming for yourself your most positive and potent direction as you work.

This is the time for reconciling opposites and bringing your wholeself into balance: LIGHT/DARK, YOUNG/OLD, FEMALE/MALE, CONSCIOUS/UNCONSCIOUS, ACTIVE/PASSIVE, MATERIAL/SPIRITUAL, etc

Pass a talking stick or wand around. Speak only when you hold the stick. Say what you are grateful for.

Clear out your living space, give away what is no longer relevant. Wash and cleanse everything, so that you begin the new phase with clarity.

SAMHAIN

END OCTOBER
BEGIN NOVEMBER

AUTUMN CROSS-QUARTER
HALLOWEEN · HALLOWS EVE ·
ALL SOULS NIGHT · DARK MOON ·
FEAST OF THE DEAD
FESTIVAL of REMEMBERANCE

THIS IS THE ENDING AND BEGINNING OF THE CELTIC
NEW YEAR, AFFIRMING REBIRTH IN THE MIDST OF
DEATH AND DARKNESS. AT SAMHAIN, (PRONOUNCED
SOW-EIN) THE GRAIN MOTHER BECOMES THE CRONE, THE
WISE WOMAN, THE DEATH ASPECT OF HER TRINITY.

SAMHAIN, LIKE BELTAIN, IS A MAGICAL TIME.
THE VEIL BETWEEN THE SEEN WORLD OF MATTER AND
THE UNSEEN WORLD OF SPIRIT BECOMES THIN,
ESPECIALLY AT DAWN AND DUSK — A CRACK IN
THE FABRIC OF SPACE TIME. IT IS A TIME FOR
COMMUNICATION WITH THE ANCESTORS, A TIME FOR
DIVINATION, OMENS, PORTENTS AND SEEKING THE
MYSTERIES. IT IS A TIME TO DRIFT, DREAM AND
VISION; A TIME FOR INNER JOURNEYS AND
CONNECTING TO THE WISDOM INSIDE YOURSELF.

THE REGENERATIVE POWER OF THIS DARK
TIME OF YEAR BECAME LOST. 'HEL' WAS ORIGINALLY
A SACRED CAVE OF REBIRTH, CONNECTED TO THE
NORSE QUEEN OF THE UNDERWORLD, HELLENES.
FEAR AND SUPERSTITION REPLACED ITS POSITIVE
ATTRIBUTES. BUT NOW, AFTER ITS LONG PERIOD OF
REST IN THE DARK, UNDERSTANDING IS RE-
EMERGING. IT IS STRENGTHENED, REJUVENATED,
CHANGED. WE ARE EMBRACING A NEW AGE OF
INTEGRATION, WHERE LIGHT AND DARK ARE BOTH
ACCEPTED AS NECESSARY PARTS OF OUR
WHOLESELVES.

UNDERLYING ENERGY of SAMHAIN

This is the Cross Quarter Festival of Autumns end and the beginning of Winter. Increasing dark and cold means we must adjust to the new season, the dark phase of the year's cycle. Now we have time to connect to our root energy, to reflect, to journey into our unconscious and the spirit realms. Now we must make time to rest. The seeds of our ideas and future direction in life are incubated now, ready for rebirth at the Solstice. This endless cycle of change is necessary, bringing renewal of ourselves, our cells, our understanding, our ideas. This cycle of death and rebirth means that there are always new opportunities to start again.

I AM
TOMORROWS ANCESTOR
THE FUTURE OF YESTERDAY
AND WHAT I AM
IN THE HERE AND NOW
GOES RIPPLING OUT
ALL WAYS
GOES RIPPLING OUT
ALWAYS

BY
BRIAN BOOTHBY

SAMHAIN CELEBRATIONS

✶ GATHER WITH FRIENDS AT THE DARK OF THE MOON. HOLD HANDS IN A CIRCLE. POUR A SPIRAL OF SALT ON THE FLOOR. WALK IN TO THE CENTRE, LEAVING BEHIND SOMETHING FROM THE OLD YEAR. PLACE NUTS AT THE CENTRE AND A LIGHTED CANDLE. TAKE A NUT, REPRESENTING A NEW SEED FOR YOU, WALK OUT OF THE SPIRAL INSPIRED WITH A NEW DIRECTION FOR THE NEW YEAR.

✶ WELCOME AND THANK THE SPIRITS OF THE ANCESTORS, YOUR GUARDIAN ANGELS, AND SPIRIT GUIDES. SHARE YOUR THOUGHTS FOR THOSE FRIENDS AND FAMILY WHO HAVE DIED, BUT DO NOT ATTEMPT TO CALL THEM BACK IN ANY WAY.

✶ A NIGHT TO LIGHT A FIRE. PLACE IN THE FIRE (AN OBJECT, SOMETHING WRITTEN ON PAPER, OR SYMBOLICALLY GIVEN TO A TWIG OR LEAF) SOMETHING YOU WISH TO TRANSFORM OR PURIFY. SPEAK IT OUT. HONOUR THE CYCLE OF ENDINGS & REBIRTH.

✶ MAKE HEAD-DRESSES, CROWNS, MASKS, OR POSIES, USING THE DYING VEGETATION FROM THE OLD YEAR. LATER BURN THEM IN THE FIRE, LETTING GO OF THE OLD YEAR AND WELCOMING THE NEW CYCLE.

✶ THE NEW CYCLE BEGINS WITH THE DARK AND TIME WITHIN. EACH EAT AN APPLE AND USE THE SEEDS TO SHARE WITH EACHOTHER WHAT YOU WISH TO INCUBATE DURING THE WINTER MONTHS — AND THEN EAT THEM!

✶ A NIGHT FOR MAKING INNER JOURNEYS, FOR FACING FEARS, CONSULTING WITH THE ANCESTORS. TAKE A RUNE, TAROT CARD, OGHAM STICK, OR ANY DIVINATION SYSTEM. ASK FOR GUIDANCE. ASK YOUR SPIRIT GUIDES TO WORK WITH YOU, TO HELP YOU ON THE SPIRITUAL PATH YOU WALK.

39.

THE MOON

The Solar year and the eight festivals connects us to the seasonal flow of the earths cycle. Interwoven within this is the lunar month (approximately 29 days). As the Moon orbits the Earth, the moon's reflective qualities bring receptivity and assimilation. The moon influences the waters of our planet and our bodies, affecting the ovulation cycles of women and animals, the growth patterns of plants and the migration patterns of birds. Her force of gravity is so powerful it causes two high tides a day.

The alternating waxing and waning of the moon's cycle also influences the watery nature of our unconsciousness, our emotions, our moods, feelings and perceptions. Her cycle influences us more deeply than most of us are aware.

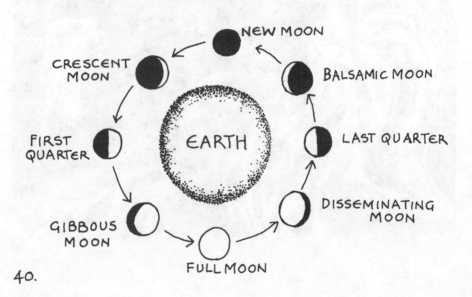

NEW MOON

CRESCENT MOON

BALSAMIC MOON

FIRST QUARTER

EARTH

LAST QUARTER

GIBBOUS MOON

DISSEMINATING MOON

FULL MOON

NEW MOON. The Sun and Moon rise together in the East. The Moon is invisible because she is hidden by the Sun's brightness. A time for new beginnings, new projects, new directions, new resolutions and seeds. It is the best time for invocation and speaking out your intent.

CRESCENT MOON. Rises mid morning and sets after sunset. Brings growth to all plans.

WAXING HALF MOON. Rises at midday and sets about midnight. Brings growth & activity.

GIBBOUS MOON. Rises just before sunset, sets just before dawn. A time of activity and expressing yourself through your feelings.

FULL MOON. Rises at sunset, sets at sunrise. A time for celebration and outward expression. Brings change, revelation, emotional peaks, heightened energy, sleepless nights.

DISSEMINATING MOON. The Moon begins to wane, rising mid-evening and setting mid-morning (one hour later after sunset each night) Brings self assessment, looking within, reflection, root growth.

WANING HALF MOON. Rises at midnight, sets at midday and is visible from when she rises to when she sets. Brings transformation, inner reflection, change.

BALSAMIC MOON (WANING CRESCENT) Rises before dawn and sets mid-afternoon. The last sliver in the eastern sky early morning. Brings inner wisdom, the dark—

41.

MYSTERIES, INNER KNOWLEDGE. THIS IS THE TIME FOR
BANISHING RITUALS, TO LET GO OF WHAT IS NO LONGER
HELPFUL TO YOU, TO BREAK PSYCHIC LINKS.

DARK OF THE MOON · SHE IS DARK FOR 3
DAYS BEFORE BECOMING NEW. USE THIS TIME FOR
GUIDANCE, UNDERSTANDING AND ASSIMILATION OF
INNER WISDOM.

FULL MOON
IN AQUARIUS

WHAT IS THIS
COMING THROUGH THE FIRE?
WHAT IS THIS SPELL IN THE SONG?
WHAT IS THIS STAR BURNING BRIGHTER?
WHAT IS THIS? WHAT IS THIS?

THERE'S A RISE IN THE EYES
OF THE GODS OF THE FOREST
THERE'S A SWELL IN THE HEART OF THE GODS OF THE SEA.
SKY-FLIERS SWIM IN THE WINDS OF THE WANTING
AND THE GODDESS FLAME BURNS READY
INVITING FOOTPRINTS ON A PATH TO THE DAWN
BEWITCHING STEPS ACROSS A LEAPING FIRE
ARMS OUTSTRETCHED IN THE LOVE OF THE MOMENT
IN THE YELL OF THE YELLING AND THE BREATH OF DESIRE

IT'S A RISING TIDE OF A NEW GENERATION
SWELLING SEA OF A STORM TO COME
SHIVER IN THE LEAVES ON A FINE SUMMER DAWN
ECHO OF THE FUTURE IN THE TRIBAL DRUM

FULL MOON, FULL MOON IN AQUARIUS.

BY BRIAN BOOTHBY

I AM ONE WITH MY PATH AGAIN AND IT IS GOOD AS LAUGHING

44.

ENDPIECE FROM A FRIEND.......

THERE IS NO SEPARATION BETWEEN US AND THE CYCLE OF LIFE AND DEATH. WE ARE IT, TOGETHER WITH THE REST OF CREATION. WE ARE THE LIFE FORCE THAT FLOWS THROUGH EVERYTHING. THE SEASONS OF THE YEAR, THE TURNING OF THE WHEEL, ARE REFLECTED IN OUR OWN LIFE OF TRANSITIONS, THROUGH BIRTH, GROWTH, SEXUALITY, MATURITY, REPRODUCTION, HARVEST, COMPLETION AND EVENTUAL RECONNECTION WITH THE SOURCE.

THE CELTS WERE NOT AFRAID OF DEATH BECAUSE THEY HAD LIVED WITH THE DYNAMIC EXPERIENCE OF THE CONTINUING CYCLE OF LIFE. AT EACH FESTIVAL THEY HAD PHYSICALLY, EMOTIONALLY INTELLECTUALLY AND SPIRITUALLY HONOURED THEMSELVES, THEIR PAST, PRESENT AND FUTURE, THEIR ANCESTORS, THEIR FAMILIES, THE LIGHT AND THE SHADOW, THEIR FEMALE AND MALENESS, CONTEXT AND CONTENT, IN BREATH AND OUTBREATH.

THEY DID NOT CONCEIVE GODDESS OR GOD AS OUTSIDE THEMSELVES. THEY LIVED CONSCIOUSLY, LOVING NATURE, KNOWING THEMSELVES TO BE PART OF IT. THEY SAW THE WAXING AND WANING OF SUN AND MOON, THROUGH THE YEAR & THE MONTH AS PART OF THEIR OWN ENERGY PATTERN AS INDIVIDUALS AND AS PART OF SOCIETY, AND CELEBRATED EACH PHASE, HONOURING ALL THE ABUNDANCE, CHALLENGES, JOY AND PAIN AS PART OF A GREAT COSMOLOGY OF THE KNOWN AND THE UNKNOWN.

OUR DYNAMIC CONNECTION WITH THE LIFE FORCE BRINGS US NEW POWER AND VIBRANCY TO EVERY ASPECT OF OUR LIVES. WE ARE PART OF A SACRED AND CREATIVE PROCESS OF LOVE AND UNDERSTANDING WHICH IS INFINITE, AND INTERCONNECTED TO ALL THAT IS.

Ann Morgan

45.

DEDICATED TO THE EARTH AND ALL OF NATURE SEEN AND UNSEEN; TO MY CHILDREN, MAY, JACK AND JERRY FOR BRINGING ME SO MUCH HAPPINESS AND MAKING ME LAUGH; AND TO MY GUARDIAN ANGELS AND SPIRIT GUIDES WHOSE CONNECTION BECOMES EVER STRONGER THE MORE I ACKNOWLEDGE THEIR PRESENCE.

MY HEARTFELT THANKS AND LOVE TO THE CELEBRATIONS GROUP AND THE ELEMENTALS FOR ALL THE SHARING AND LOVE OF OUR EVER DEEPENING FRIENDSHIPS; AND TO MY PARTNER BRIAN BOOTHBY FOR HIS LOVE AND ALL THE WONDERFUL SONGS HE WRITES, SOME OF WHICH ARE INCLUDED IN THIS BOOK AND ARE AVAILABLE ON CD OR TAPE FROM PUBLISHER'S ADDRESS.

PLEASE SEND S.A.E TO PUBLISHER'S ADDRESS FOR DETAILS OF OTHER PUBLICATIONS, CARDS AND PRINTS.

GLENNIE KINDRED IS AVAILABLE FOR WORKSHOPS, TALKS, FACILITATING GROUP CELEBRATIONS AND CREATING SACRED GARDENS BOTH PERMANENT AND TEMPORARY.

OTHER BOOKS BY GLENNIE KINDRED
SEND S.A.E. FOR DETAILS TO : LEAMOOR · DERBY RD
WIRKSWORTH · DERBYSHIRE. DE4 4AR.

THE SACRED TREE   ISBN · 0-9532227-1-3

An exploration of 13 native trees in the circle of the year. Celtic Tree-lore, folklore, herbal uses, uses of the wood, spiritual and healing properties of each tree, communicating with tree spirits.

THE TREE OGHAM   ISBN· 0-9532227-2-1

An ancient system used by the Druids, explored here as an aid to self-healing and spiritual development, communicating with trees and making your own Ogham sticks which can be used for connecting to divine inspiration and inner knowledge.

CREATING CEREMONY   ISBN· 0-9532227-4-8

Co-written with Lu Garner, A self-help guide to creating ceremony for all occasions: baby welcoming, puberty, marriage, joinings, separations, funerals, loss, rites of passage, moon cycles, cleansing, space clearing, daily rituals and more. Inspiring you to confidently mark and honour the events in your life.

HERBAL HEALERS   ISBN · 1-902418-09-3

21 familiar, common and easy to recognise herbs, their comprehensive medicinal uses both for 1st aid and common ailments. Includes gathering and drying times, dosage guides, internal and external herbal preparations and a repertory.

HEDGEROW COOKBOOK ISBN: 1-902418-11-5

A SEASONAL GUIDE TO GATHERING, COOKING AND STORING, SAFE AND EASY TO RECOGNISE WILD FOOD.

SACRED CELEBRATIONS
A SOURCE BOOK. ISBN: 0-906362-48-2

A GREATLY EXPANDED EDITION OF 'THE EARTH'S CYCLE OF CELEBRATION.' SUBJECTS INCLUDE: THE FIVE ELEMENTS, THE RHYTHMS OF THE MOON, EARTH ENERGY AND SACRED LANDSCAPE, INNER JOURNEYING, MEDITATION, DANCE, SONG, MASK AND MASK MAKING, THE HEALING ENERGIES OF TREES AND HERBS, CELEBRATIONS FOR CHILDREN, CRAFT RELATED ACTIVITIES, GARDEN AND LAND PROJECTS, LABYRINTH MAKING, BUILDING A SWEAT LODGE, CREATING SACRED SPACE BOTH INSIDE AND OUTSIDE, AND MANY OTHER CREATIVE ACTIVITIES TO ENHANCE AND CONNECT TO THE MOMENT, THE EARTH'S CYCLES AND TO EACHOTHER.

EACH OF THE 8 FESTIVALS ARE EXPLORED IN DEPTH AND LOTS OF IDEAS AND SUGGESTIONS MADE FOR PREPARING FOR, AND CELEBRATING, BOTH ON YOUR OWN OR WITH A GROUP.

CD's AND CASSETTES:

TOMORROWS ANCESTOR - BY BRIAN BOOTHBY

FULL MOON - BY BRIAN BOOTHBY AND TOMORROWS ANCESTOR.

CARDS AND PRINTS OF THE ILLUSTRATIONS.